CW01667771

Year 1
Textbook

Pearson

Published by Pearson Education Limited, 80 Strand, London, WC2R 0RL.
www.pearson.com/international-schools

Copies of official specifications for all Pearson Edexcel qualifications may be found on the website:
https://qualifications.pearson.com

Text © Pearson Education Limited 2023
Produced by Just Content Ltd
Designed by PDQ Media Digital Media Solutions
Typeset by PDQ Media Digital Media Solutions
Picture research by © Straive Ltd
Original illustrations © Pearson Education Limited 2023
Cover design © Pearson Education Limited 2023

First published 2023

26 25 24
10 9 8 7

British Library Cataloguing in Publication Data
A catalogue record for this book is available from the British Library

ISBN 978 1 292 43342 4

Printed in the UK by Bell & Bain

Contents

Welcome to Pearson International Primary Science!

This book is a key part of your journey to becoming a young scientist.

Let's take a look at some of the features.

Introduction
This introduces you to what the lesson is about.

Information
These are some of the important things you will learn in the lesson.

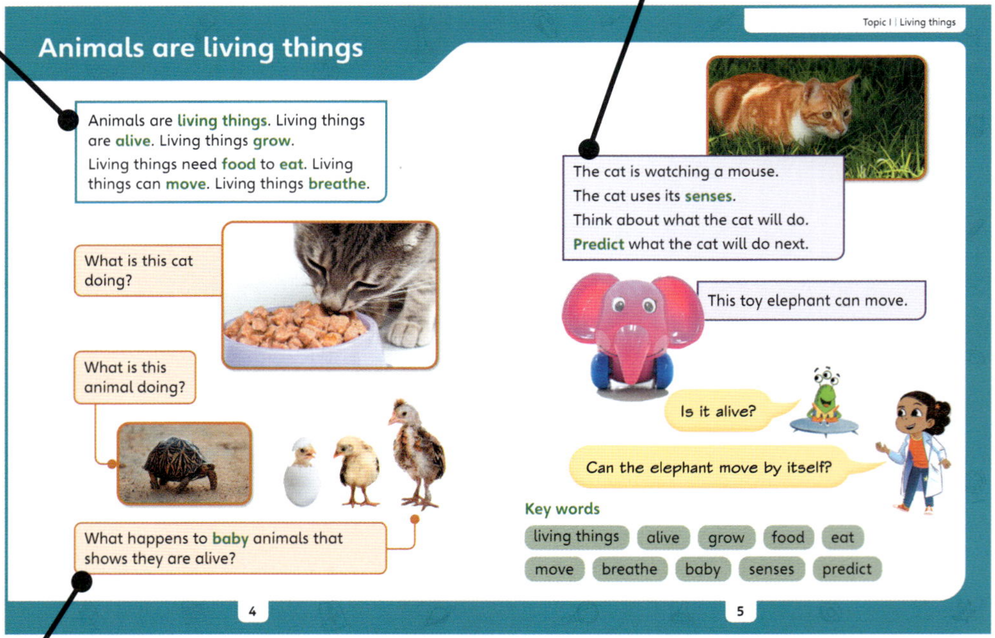

Questions
There are lots of questions within the lesson to challenge your thinking.

Key words

These are important words to know. They are highlighted in green in the lesson.

Mascots

There are helpful hints and questions from our mascots.

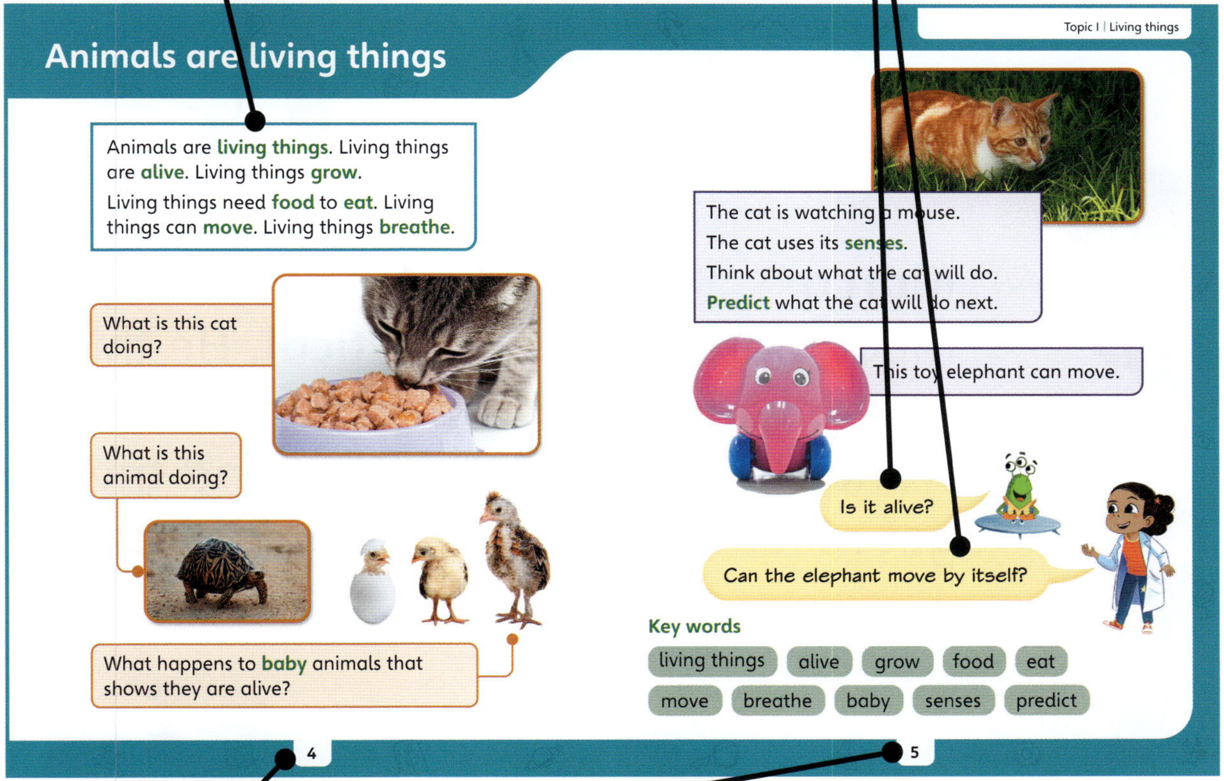

Page numbers

The page numbers for each lesson exactly match the page numbers in your workbook. This means you can easily find the workbook page for every textbook lesson.

Meet the mascots

Asha

This is Asha. She is good at science and helps others to **understand** things. Asha works **accurately** and will help you to do that too.

Marco

Meet Marco! He is **analytical**. He thinks carefully about how things in the world work. He likes **investigating** and tries to get reliable results by doing fair tests.

Victor the giant tortoise

Say hello to Victor. He is a giant tortoise from the Galapagos Islands. Victor is 120 years old! Victor is **observant** and keen to explore the world beyond his island.

Sully the gull

Wave hello to Sully. He is a type of bird called a gull. Gulls can be found all over the world! He is **curious**. Sully can fly up high or swoop down low to question things from different viewpoints.

Zorp the alien

This is Zorp! Zorp enjoys **exploring**. Zorp knows a lot about our Solar System and likes to share that knowledge.

And finally ... you!

You are a very important part of these books. We hope you enjoy exploring and investigating science, asking lots of questions and having fun!

Project skills

Using a reference book: contents pages

A book is usually divided into parts called chapters. At the front of the book are pages called contents pages. A contents page shows you the order of the chapters and the pages they start and end on.

Activity

This is a book about plants.
Look at the chapters.

1. Trees and bushes
2. Flowering plants
3. Desert plants
4. Growing plants in pots
5. Fruit trees

Which chapters are about trees?
Which chapter is about growing plants?

Find a book and look at the contents page. Ask a partner to find the start of a chapter you can see on the contents page.

Now look at the chapters with the page numbers.

How does having the page numbers help?

Activity

Think about why the page numbers start on page 2.

Which chapter has the most pages?

Find another book and look at the contents page. Challenge your partner to find the last page of each chapter quickly.

1 Living things

The world is full of living things.
Let us look at some of them together.

Humans are living things.

Plants and animals are living things.

Some things, like sticks, were once alive.

Some things, like rocks, are non-living.

What living things can you see in the picture?

Animals are living things

Animals are **living things**.
Living things are **alive**. Living things **grow**.
Living things need **food** to **eat**.
Living things can **move**. Living things **breathe**.

What is this cat doing?

What is this animal doing?

What happens to **baby** animals that shows they are alive?

The cat is watching a mouse.

The cat uses its **senses**.

Think about what the cat will do.

Predict what the cat will do next.

This toy elephant can move.

Is it alive?

Can the elephant move by itself?

Key words

living things | alive | grow | food | eat

move | breathe | baby | senses | predict

Plants are living things

Plants are **living** things. Plants are alive.

The picture shows a small plant changing.
What is the plant doing?

Can plants move?

Plants move by **growing**.

These bean plants move by growing around sticks.

These plants are growing towards a window. They need **sunlight** to make food.

So plants make food?

Yes, they make their food using sunlight. That is why most plants are **green**.

Look at these plants.

They take **air** in and out but we do not call it breathing.

Plants have tiny holes in their leaves. Air can go in and out of the plant.

Key words

living | growing | sunlight | green | air

Living or non-living?

Some things are alive. Some things are **non-living**. They are not alive.

Look at this picture.
The woman is alive. She is a living thing. The table is not alive. It is a non-living thing.

Look for more living and non-living things in the pictures.

How did you decide which are the living things?

Discuss with your partner to share your ideas.

This plant is alive.

This is the same plant.

Is it alive now?

Living things die. **Dead** things used to be alive.

This spider is alive. There are some dead flies on the spider's web. Predict what the spider will do with the dead flies.

Key words

non-living dead

Are robots alive?

Humans make **machines** that can do some of the things that living things can do.

These **robot** arms are making cars. The robot arms can move.

What is making the robot arms move? Can they move by themselves?

This tea farmer is using drones to look after the tea plants. The drones can fly.

How do the drones know where to fly?

These robot arms are packing boxes.

How do the robot arms know what to put into the boxes?

This robot looks like a living thing. It can help people. It can talk. It can move. Is it alive?

No, the robot cannot breathe or grow. It cannot do all the things that living things do.

Key words

machines

robot

Animals grow and change

Living things grow. They **change** as they grow. A grown-up animal is called an **adult**. Adult animals have **offspring**. The offspring are called babies.

baby monkey

Which monkey is **younger**?

adult monkey

What makes the adult monkey look **older**?

The adult monkey is a **parent** of the baby monkey.

Animals that have fur or hair can make milk to feed their babies.

Sometimes we give the adult animals and the baby animals different names.

Baby gulls are called chicks.

These babies are called cubs. Do the cubs look like the adults?

This is a kitten. What does it grow into?

caterpillar

butterfly

Some baby animals do not look like the adult.

Look for three differences between this adult and baby animal.

Key words

change | adult | offspring | younger | older | parent

Watching plants grow and change

Plants are living things. Living things grow. Plants change as they grow.

These are **beans**. Humans can eat these beans.

We can plant beans. The beans grow into new plants. The new plants make more beans.

Living things can make new living things.

Try growing a bean into a plant.

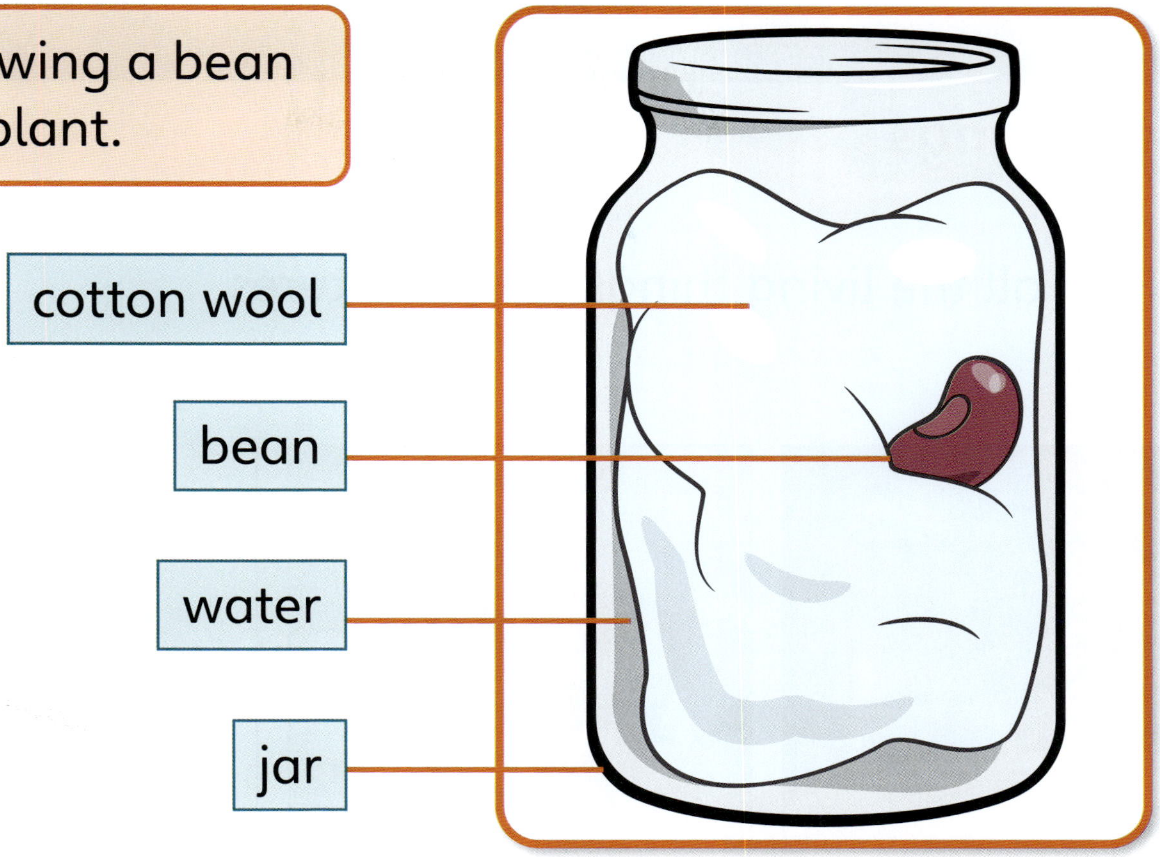

Choose a tall bottle or jar that lets **sunlight** in for the bean.

The bean needs sunlight, air and **water**. It has its own food, inside the bean.

Look at your bean every day. Can you see it changing? You could draw pictures of your bean as it grows.

Key words

beans sunlight water

End of topic questions

Living things

1. Find all the living things in the pictures.

2 Write a list of what all living things can do.
Use the pictures below to help you start.

2 Myself

Humans are living things. You are a human, and your family and friends are humans.

We all look different, but we have many things that are the same.

Humans have a head with sense organs and a mouth to eat food.

Humans have arms and legs joined to a body.

Humans can breathe, move, eat and grow. This shows that they are living things.

Humans grow and change as they get older.

Humans are living things

Humans are living things. These humans are alive.

Find all the adults in the picture.

The adults have been alive for **longer** than the children.

What is this baby **drinking**?

How many years has the baby been alive?

How many years have you been alive?

Why is the baby sucking the drink?

Most newborn babies do not have teeth. They only drink **milk**.

Then they start to eat soft food.

What is this baby doing that shows she is alive?

Is this baby alive?

What is he doing?

Key words

longer | children | drinking | milk

Staying alive

Humans need food, water and air to stay alive. We get some of our water from food.

Watermelon contains a lot of water.

Which of these foods do you think contains more water?

toasted bread

cucumber

Air is all around us. We do not see it but we know it is there.

These children are blowing out air.

Breathe onto a mirror or a window.

Can you see the water in the air you **breathe out**?

We need air to breathe.

We breathe air in and we breathe air out.

The air we breathe out has water from our body in it.

Key words

breathe out

Five senses

We use our senses to find out about the world around us. We have five **sense organs**.

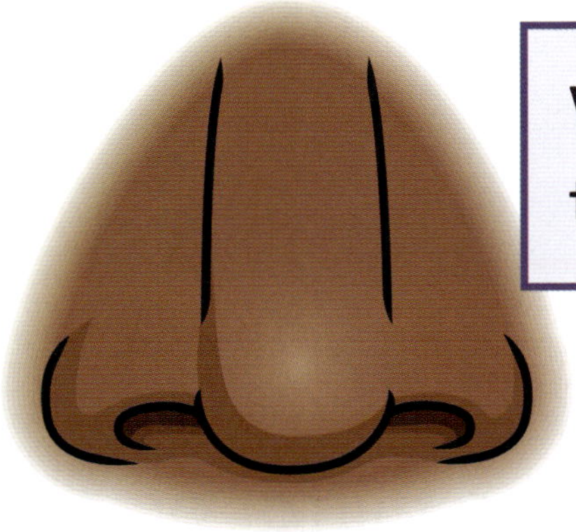

We use our **nose** to **smell** things.

smell

taste

We use our **tongue** to **taste** things.

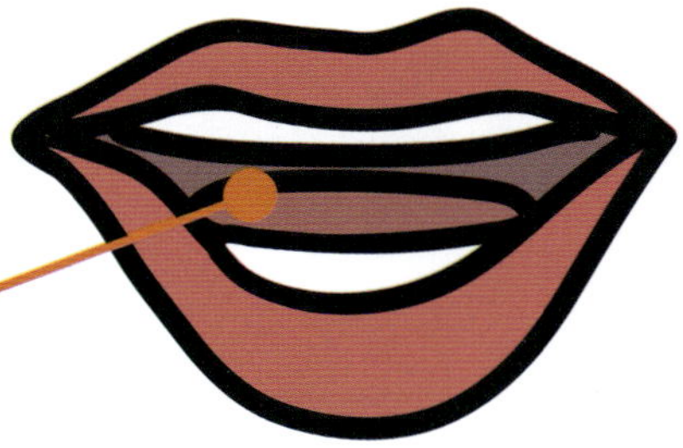

We use our **eyes** to **see** things.

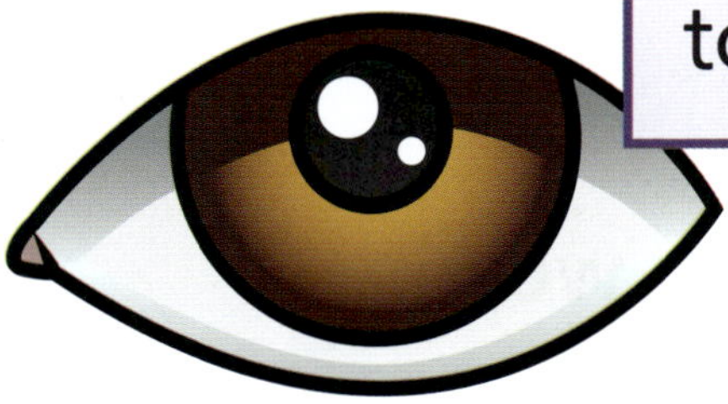

sight

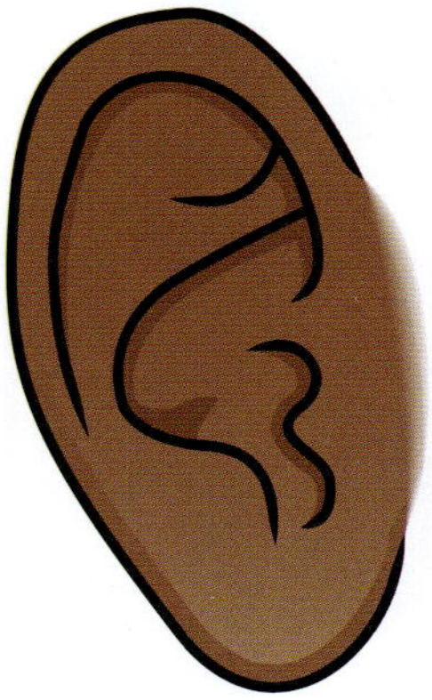

We use our **ears** to **hear** things.

We use our **skin** to **touch** things.

This person is **feeling** a prickly cactus plant.

Which sense organ is she using?

Key words

sense organs | nose | smell | tongue | taste

eyes | see | ears | hear | skin | touch | feeling

Seeing things

Humans have two eyes. We use our eyes to **look** at things.

Where is the thing that this boy is looking at?

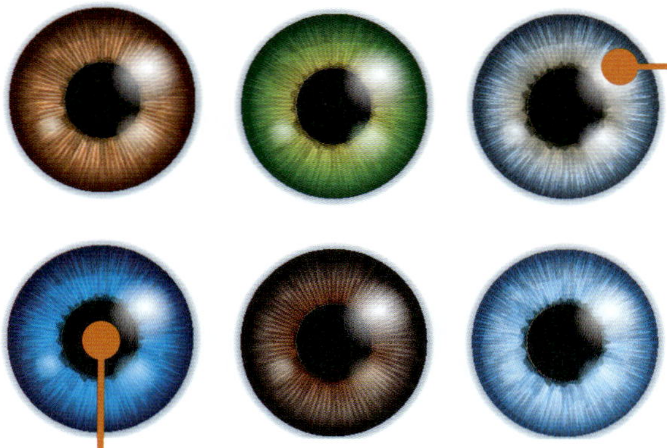

Look at your eyes in a mirror.

What colour is this part of your eye?

This is the **pupil**, where light goes into your eye.

The pupil can be big or small at different times.

We use our eyes to see.
This sense is called **sight**.

Try drawing your eye or your partner's eye.

Sometimes we can be tricked by things we look at.

Which line is longer?

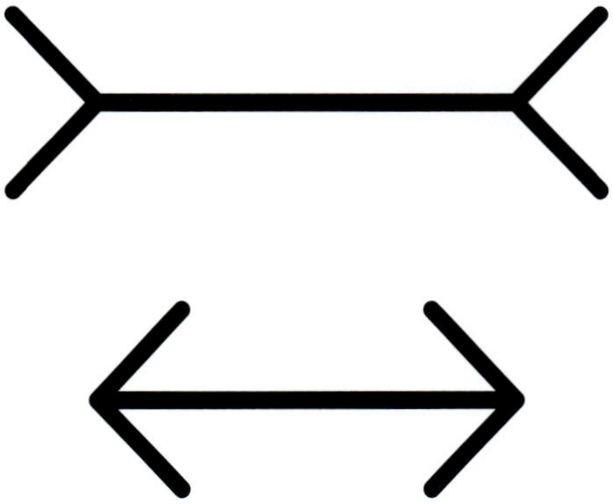

Does each zebra have a **head**?

Key words

look pupil sight head

Smell

We use our nose to smell things.

Smelling food helps to keep us **safe**.

Which food is safe to eat or drink?

Smelling the world around us can keep us safe.

Which part of the fire can we smell before we see the flames?

Nice smells can make us **happy**.

What smells are shown in the pictures?

Which pictures show nice smells?

How can I smell like a scientist?

Scientists wave smells towards their nose. There are lots of chemicals that might damage the inside of their noses.

Key words

safe happy

Taste

We use our tongue to taste things. Taste buds on the surface help us to find out what food tastes like.

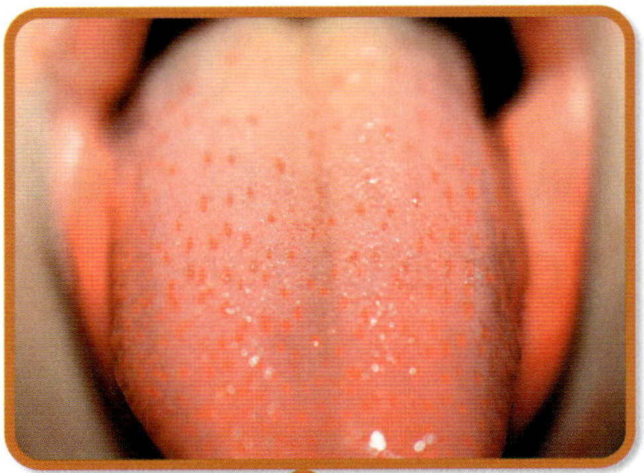

Use a mirror to look at the surface of your tongue.

We also use **smell** to help us taste food. Look at how the chef waves the smell to his nose before tasting it.

Food that is going bad does not taste very nice.

Our tongue senses **different** flavours. This helps us to find out what different foods taste like.

Key words

smell different

I like the taste of salty fish.
Which tastes do you like best?

Hearing

We use our ears to hear **sounds**.

This girl is listening.

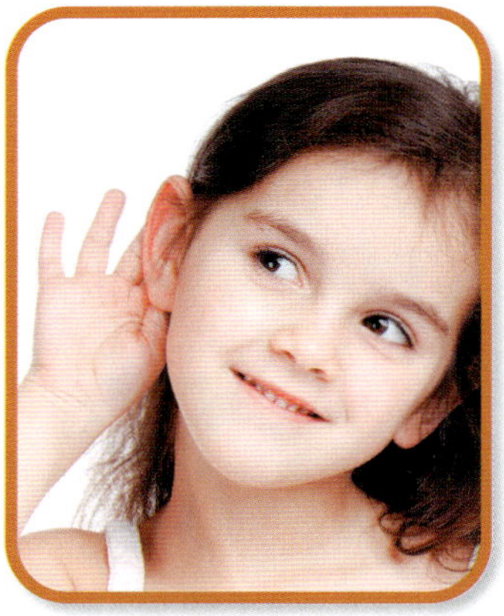

What do you think the people in the pictures are **listening** to?

What sounds can they hear?

Close your eyes and listen.
What sounds can you hear?

Where are the sounds coming from?

Use a mirror to look at your ears.

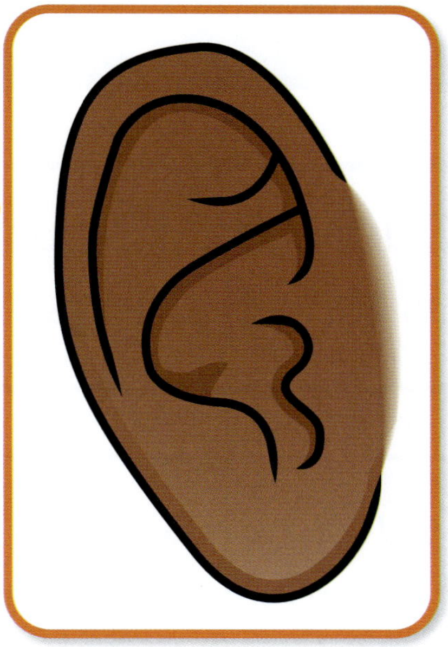

The part you can see is your outer ear. The rest of your ear is inside your head.

Some animals can move their outer ear to find the direction of a sound.

This cat can move its ears.

Key words

sounds listening

Touch

Our sense of touch helps us to feel things.

Touch helps us to find out if things are **hot** or **cold**.

We can find this button in the dark by feeling with our **fingers**.

This is because different surfaces have different **textures**.

People who cannot see may read books using touch.

This is called Braille.

The texture of the page shows patterns of letters.

Different patterns of dots show different letters.

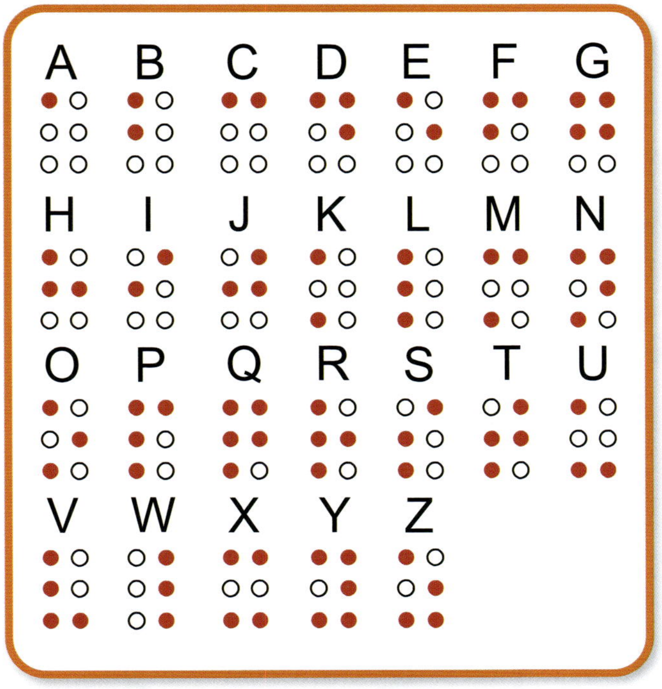

Which letters use five dots?

Why do humans use **hands** to feel things?

Where do you think your hand is most sensitive to touch?

Human hands are more **sensitive** to touch than **arms** or **legs**.

Key words

hot | cold | fingers | textures | hands | sensitive | arms | legs

Body parts

Some parts of our body are on the outside.
We can see them.

- **mouth**
- eye
- hand
- ear
- **foot**
- nose
- head
- **knee**
- **neck**
- arm

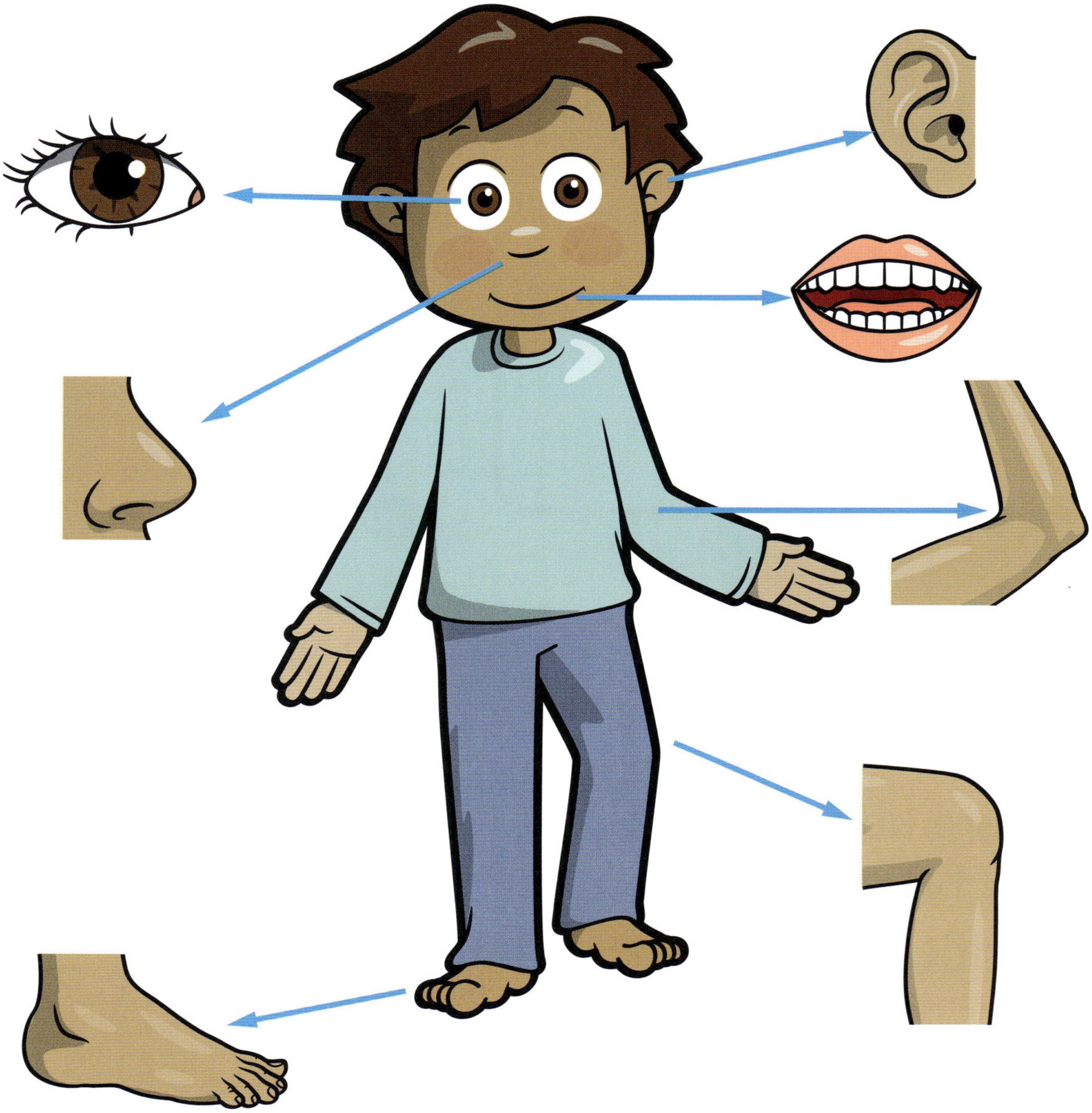

Find these body parts on the picture above.

Look at your hands.
Find these parts on your hands.

Which finger is **longest**?
Which finger is **shortest**?

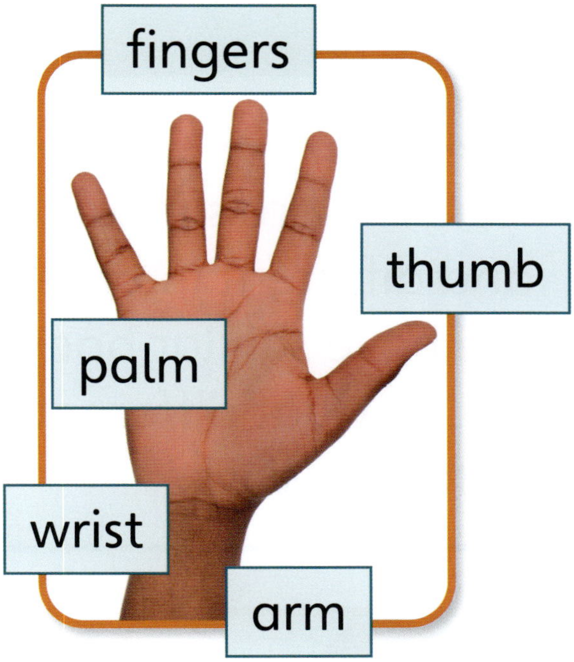

Look at your feet. Find these parts on your foot.

Which **toe** is longest?
Which toe is shortest?

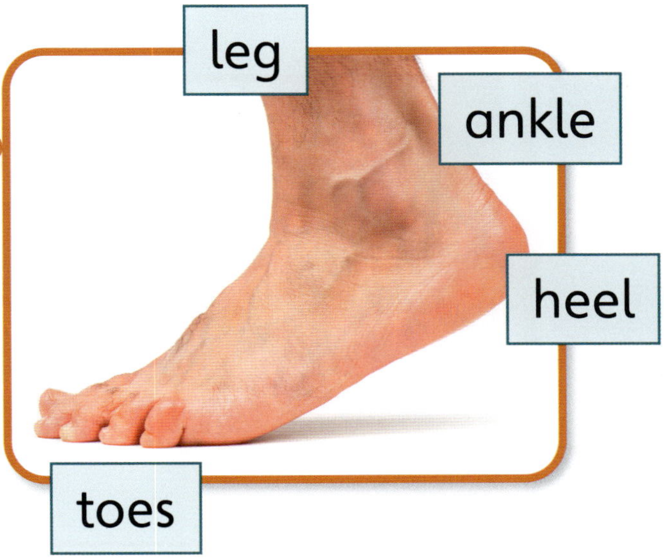

How are your hands and feet **similar**?
How do they differ?

Key words

mouth | foot | knee | neck
longest | shortest | toe | similar

Similar or different

Humans are similar in some ways and different in other ways. We have similar body parts but we may eat different things in different ways.

Which body parts do the children use to eat with?

Find someone in the pictures with:

long hair	straight hair	open mouth

Put your arm like this on a table.

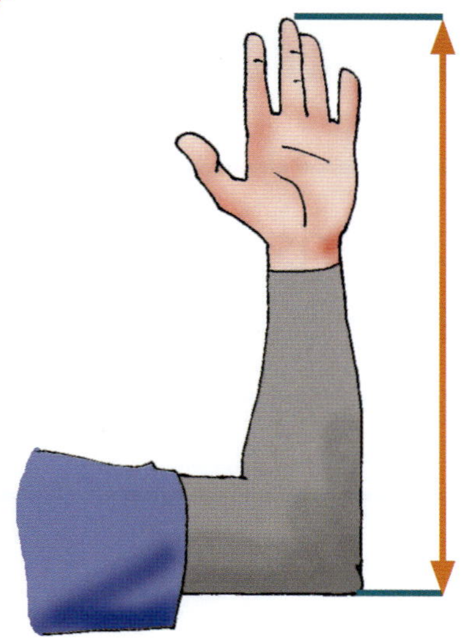

Ask someone to measure from the top of your middle finger to your elbow.

How do these measurements differ between people in your class?

People use hand spans to measure things.

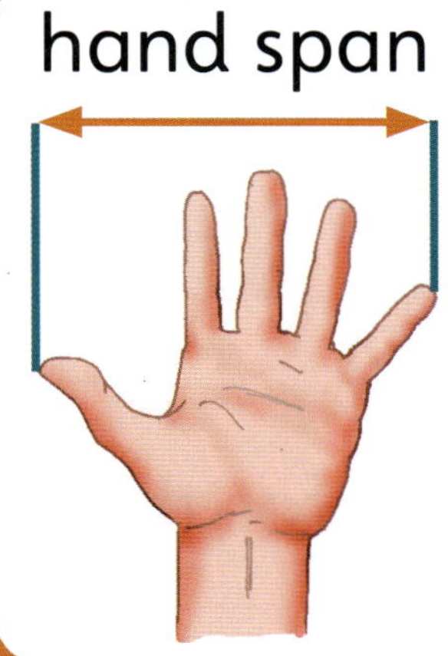

The length of a hand span differs. Most adults have bigger hand spans than children.

Humans grow and change

Humans are living things. All living things grow. When humans grow, some things look similar to when they were younger.

Look for things that change.

Look for things that stay the same.

A human starts life as a baby. The baby grows into an adult.

Babies can do everything that living things do.

But they need help to do some of them.

This is what I looked like as a baby.

You hatched out of an egg in a nest, Victor. Humans do not lay eggs.

Sometimes older people need help with things they could do when they were younger.

End of topic questions

Myself

1 Find all the living things in this office.

2 Find the names of the six body parts in the grid.

Words may be →, ←, ↑ or ↓.

nose legs eyes feet arms head

a	b	n	o	s	e
r	r	l	v	y	g
m	m	s	m	e	l
s	h	e	a	d	e
t	f	y	n	a	g
t	e	e	f	r	s

3 Animals

There are many different animals.
Let us see what some of them look like.

Scientists group living things.
Animals are one big group.
Some animals have backbones.
Some animals also have fur or feathers.

This animal has fur.
How does its fur help it to hide?

What is a vertebrate?

Scientists sort living things into different **groups**. Here is an example of two groups you have met already.

animals

plants

Scientists sort all the animals into smaller groups. They sort plants like this too.

You may see shapes sorted into groups in maths.

They are all shapes, but some are more similar to one another than others.

One group of animals all have a **backbone**.

Feel down your back with your hand.

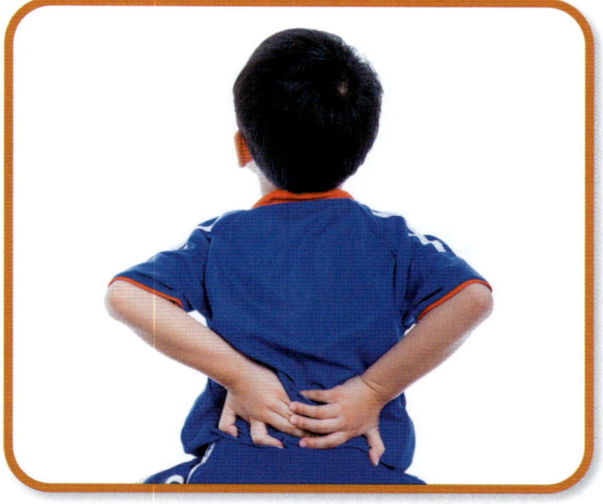

Can you feel the bumps under your skin where your backbone is?

This picture shows a human backbone, also called our **spine**. It is made of small bones called vertebrae.

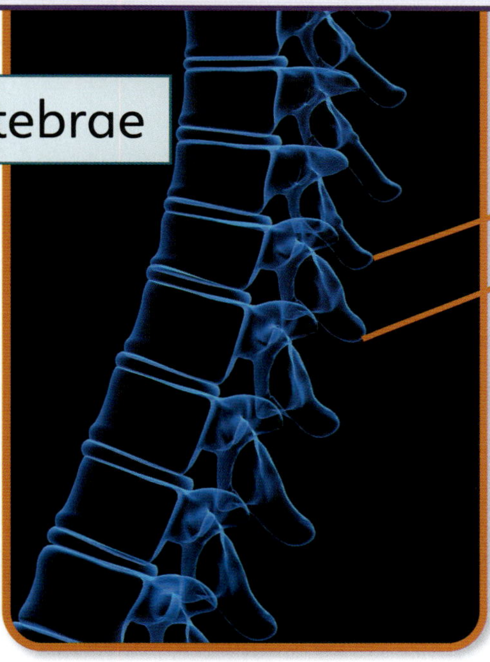

These are the bumps you can feel under your skin.

Humans are **vertebrates** because we have a backbone made of bones called vertebrae.

Key words

scientists | groups | backbone | spine | vertebrates

Vertebrate groups

All vertebrates have a backbone.

Some vertebrates have feathers and **wings**.

These are **birds**. Birds **lay eggs**.

Some vertebrates have fur or hair.

These are **mammals**. Mammals have **milk** to feed their babies.

Some vertebrates have thin, **moist** skin.

These are **amphibians**. Amphibians live on land but go to water to lay eggs.

Some vertebrates have dry skin with **scales**.

These are **reptiles**. Reptiles lay eggs on land.

Some vertebrates have scales and live in water.

These are **fish**. Most fish lay eggs in the water where they live. They have fins and a tail to help them swim.

Key words

wings | birds | lay | eggs | mammals | milk

moist | amphibians | scales | reptiles | fish

What is a key?

A key or **identification key** is a set of questions we use to help us to identify things.

We can use a key to identify an animal or plant.

The questions must have 'yes' or 'no' for the answer.

We can identify these four animals using a key.

Look at animal A. Now look at the top question in the key below.

Does animal A have feathers? Yes, it does.

Now answer the question under the 'yes' stick.

Now you can identify the animal.

Do the same for animals B, C and D.

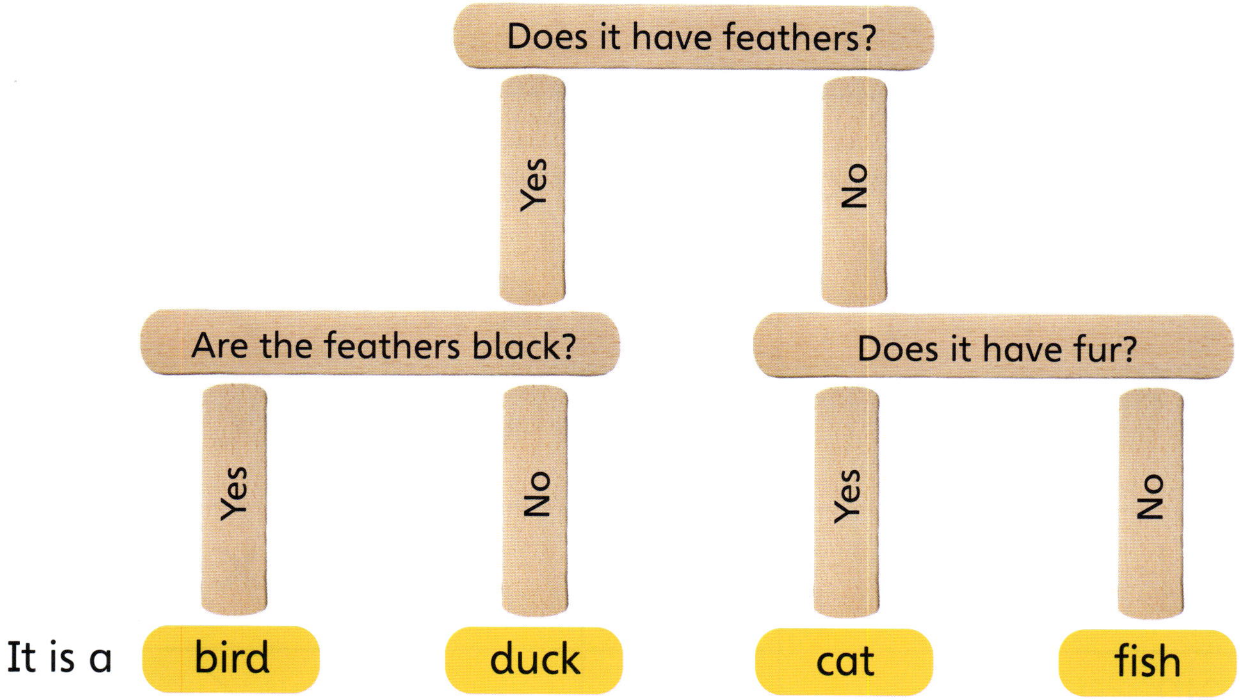

It looks like you needed three questions to identify four animals.

Key words

identification key

Differences between vertebrate groups

Scientists use identification keys to sort vertebrates into groups. This is how to make a key.

Think of questions that have yes (✓) or no (×) answers.

Make sure the answer to one question is 'yes' for more than one group.

Does it…	mammal 	bird 	reptile 	amphibian 	fish 
lay eggs on land?	✗	✓	✓	✗	✗
have feathers?	✗	✓	✗	✗	✗
have thin, moist skin?	✗	✗	✗	✓	✗
make milk for its babies?	✓	✗	✗	✗	✗

Which question has ticks for more than one group? **Ask this question first** in the identification key.

This could be bird or reptile. Now ask a new question that **splits** these two groups.

This could be mammal or amphibian or fish. Ask a new question to split these three.

This could be mammal or fish but we have not used the last question yet.

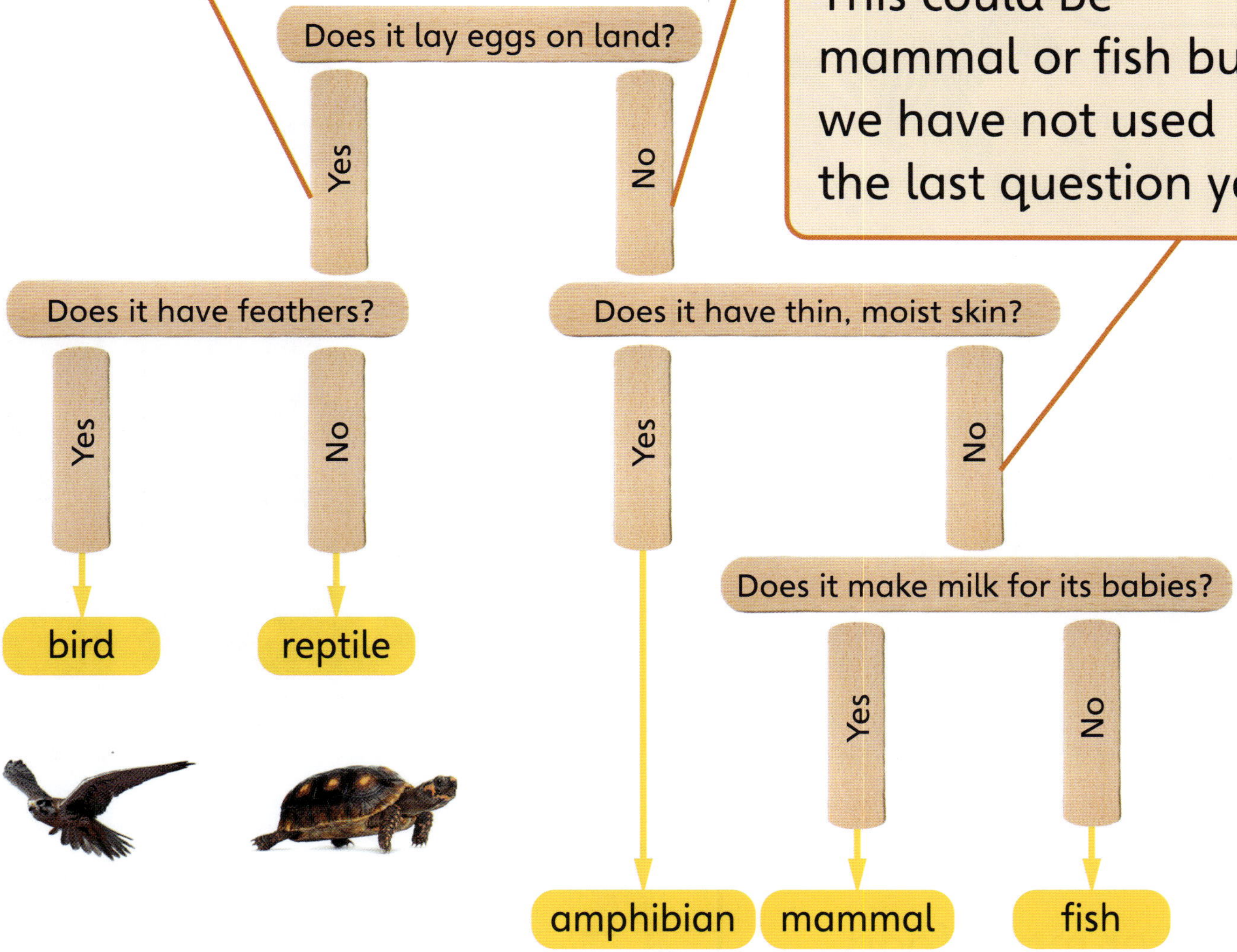

Key words

ask splits

Life processes

In the first topic you learned about living and non-living things. Can you remember what living things can do?

1. Move.

2. Use air.

3. Make more living things.

4. Grow.

5. Feed or make food. This is called **nutrition**.

6. Use senses.

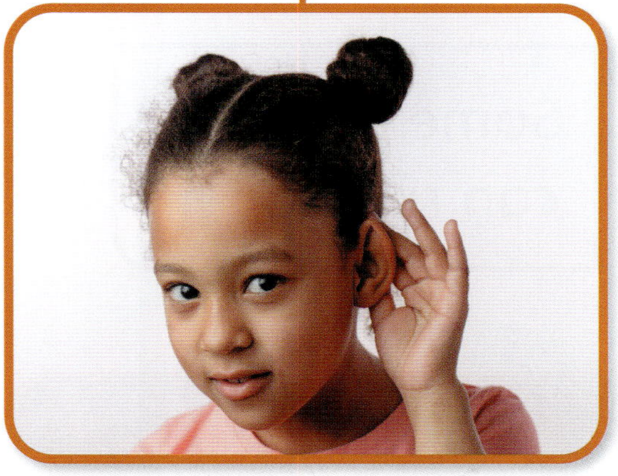

7. Living things also remove waste.

These seven things are called **life processes**.
All living things can do all seven of these life processes.

Key words

nutrition
life processes

Animals move in different ways

When animals move, they change position or go to another place. Movement is a life process.

Some animals can run.

Suggest why these zebras are **running**.

What does 'suggest' mean?

It means 'think of something for yourself'.

But do not just guess.
A suggestion is a sensible idea.

These elephants are **walking**.

Suggest why they are walking not running.

These animals are **climbing**.

Suggest why this animal is climbing the tree.

Do you think this baby animal is moving?

Kangaroos move by **jumping**.

Suggest how the kangaroo's legs help it to jump.

Key words

running walking climbing jumping

Animals grow

When animals grow they **increase** in **size**.
Growing is a life process.

In this picture, we can see how a kitten grows.
The **smallest** one is when the kitten was youngest.

When kittens grow, each part of the kitten grows.

Its ears grow **bigger**.
Its legs grow longer.

Look at these pictures of a lion cub growing.

Which parts increase in size as they grow?

Look! This is me when I was 1 month old.

You have changed colour.

I was very fluffy then. Now I have long tail feathers.

Some animals change more than others when they grow.

Animals that start life in an egg often change more than mammal babies.

Baby mammals grow and change a lot **before** they are born.

Key words

increase | size | smallest | bigger

Big eggs and small eggs

Birds lay eggs.

Baby birds **hatch** from the eggs.

Different **types** of bird lay eggs of a different size.

These are the eggs of four different birds.

When scientists look carefully at things they **observe** them.

Scientists **compare** things by observing how they are similar and how they differ.

Here are the same eggs.

Make some observations about these eggs.

How are they similar? How do they differ?

Are they easier to compare now? If so, why?

What about measuring around the eggs? Where do I measure?

Can you **measure** the height of each egg?

You must measure around the same place on each egg.

Key words

hatch types observe compare measure

Birds grow and change

Birds **lay** their eggs on land. They usually make a **nest** to keep their eggs safe.

This is a duck's nest.

How many eggs are there?

Birds' eggs have **hard shells**.

The baby bird inside can crack the shell with its **beak** when it is ready to hatch.

Baby ducks are called **ducklings**.

Here are the ducklings with their **mother**.

How have the ducklings changed?

How do they differ from the adult?

This is the **father** of the ducklings.

How do his feather colours differ from the mother duck?

Can you see a place where both adults have blue feathers?

Key words

lay | nest | hard | shells | beak | ducklings | mother | father

Reptiles

Most types of reptile lay eggs. They lay their eggs on land.

These turtles swim in the sea. They come to a beach to lay eggs in the sand.

These crocodile eggs are in a nest.

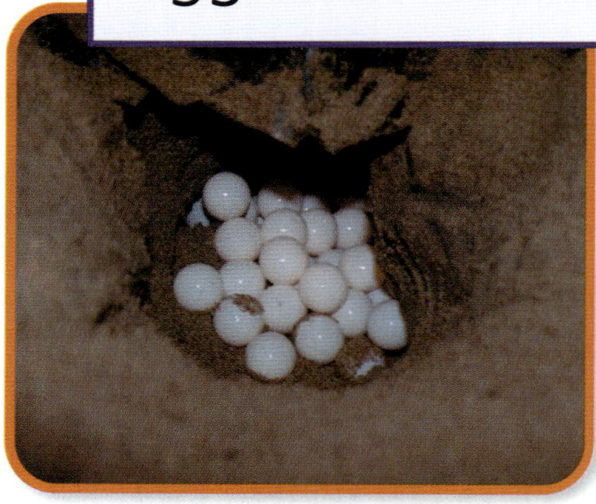

The baby crocodile looks like a tiny adult crocodile.

Can you see **teeth** and scales?

Baby crocodiles grow into adults. The adults make more eggs. Which life process is this?

Look at this diagram. Scientists call this sort of drawing a **life cycle**.

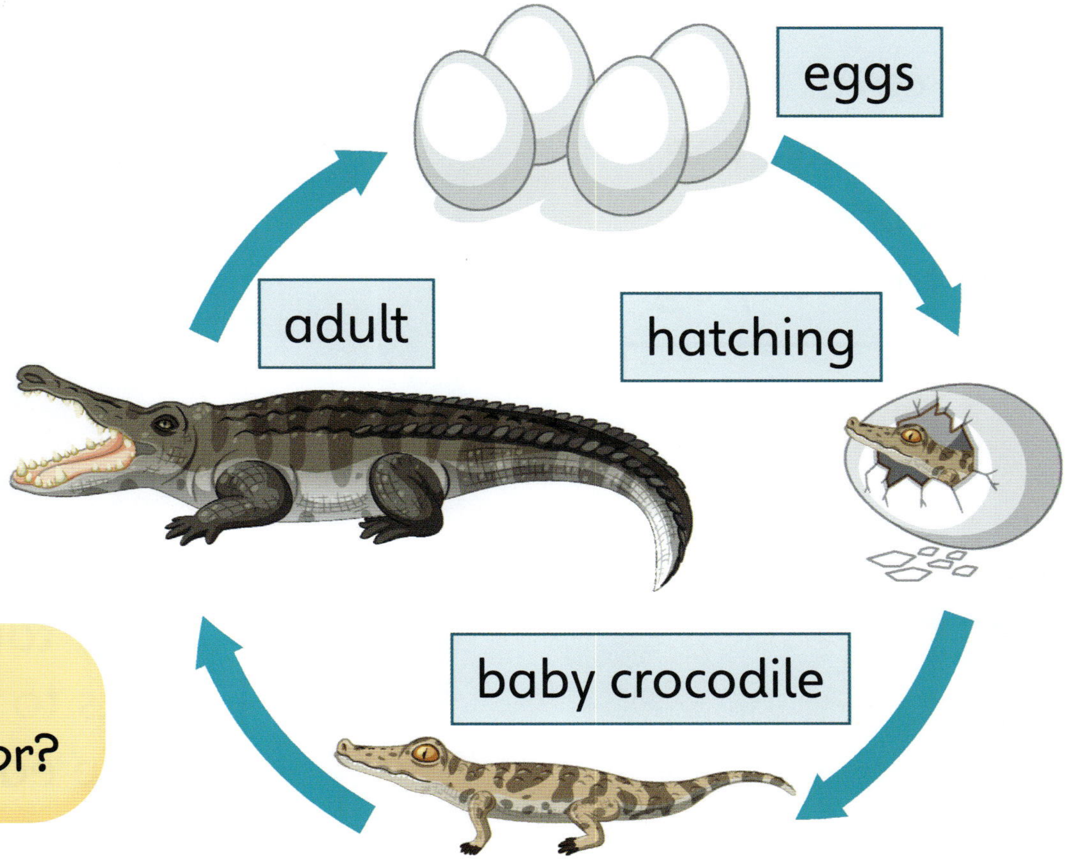

Are you a reptile, Victor?

Key words

teeth

life cycle

Yes, look at page 41 to see me hatching.

Amphibians

Amphibians lay their eggs in water. The adults may live on land but they return to a wet place to lay eggs.

These are frogs' eggs.

Frogs cover their eggs in **jelly**. The jelly **protects** the eggs from **drying**.

A tiny **tadpole** starts to grow inside each egg.

The tadpoles swim in water when they are bigger.

Tadpoles start to change into adult frogs.

This is the life cycle of a frog.

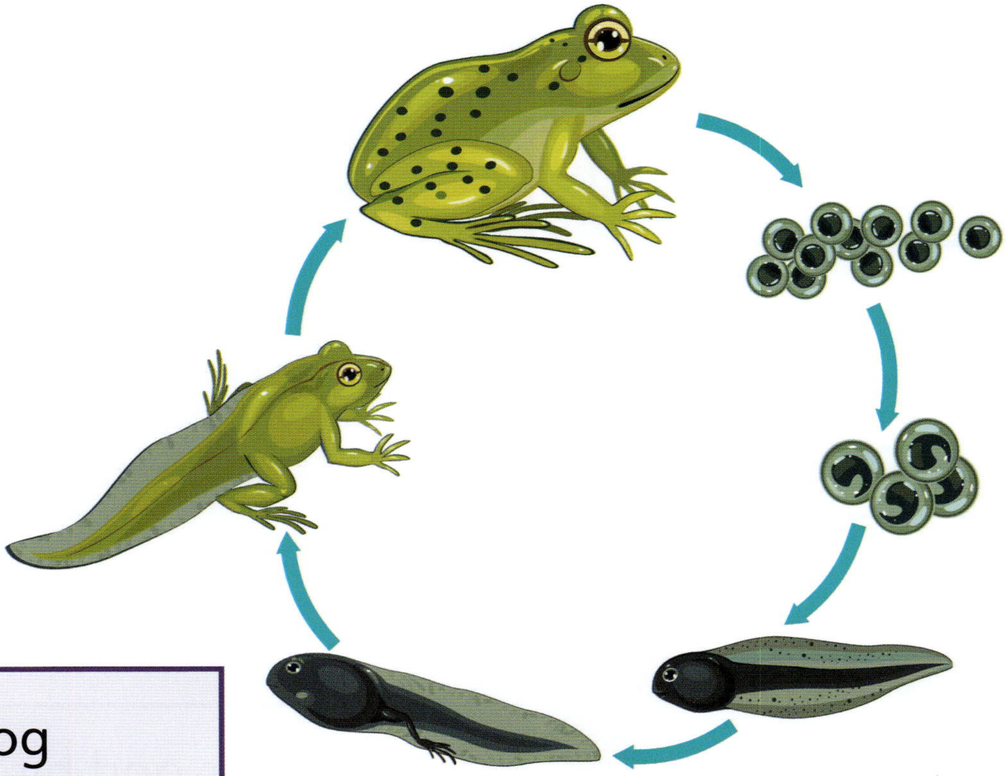

The frog changes from egg to adult.

What changes can you see?

When amphibians grow into adults they change more than reptiles change.

This is because adult amphibians live on land but their tadpoles live in water.

Key words

jelly protects drying tadpole

Nutrition

Nutrition is a life process. All animals need to eat food to stay alive.

Animals need to eat food …
to be able to move.

Mammals and birds are **warm-blooded**.

Mammals and birds need to eat food …
to stay warm.

Animals need to eat food …
to help them grow.

Adult animals can make more animals. They use the food they eat to do this.

Many adult animals feed their babies.

Mammals give their babies milk.

The milk is made using food that the mother eats.

Which of the animals on these pages are mammals?

Which are birds?

I wonder if all animals feed their babies?

Key words

warm-blooded

Eating and moving

All animals need food. Different animals have different **diets**. An animal's diet is the type of food it usually eats.

Giant pandas only eat bamboo plants.

Koalas mainly eat one type of plant too, called eucalyptus.

They do not move very much.

Giant pandas and koalas have to eat a lot of plants to stay alive.

Hummingbirds drink nectar.
Nectar is a sugary liquid inside flowers.

Hummingbirds need to use their food very quickly to be able to fly and hover.

A hummingbird drinking nectar is a bit like a footballer having an energy drink.

Key words

diets

Different diets

Many animals only eat plants, but they eat different types of plant.

This makes it easier to find food.

These giraffes are eating leaves from a tree.

This rabbit is eating grass.

I just eat plants.

Some animals only eat other animals.

They may need to move quickly to catch their food.

Some animals eat both animals and plants.

What are these black bears eating?

I like fish but I eat other food too.
I can fly to look for it.

End of topic questions

Animals

1 To which animal groups do the animals on this page belong?

2 a) Can you name some of the animals?

b) Try to find out any names you do not know.

4 Plants

Plants can be very big or quite small.
They can live for a year or for hundreds of years.

Let us find out more about the variety of plants in our world.

Most plants are green.

Some plants have bigger leaves than others.

Many plants have flowers, but some do not.

Some plants are tall and woody – we call these trees.

This flower is called a donkey orchid.

Can you see the petals that look like a donkey's ears?

Parts of a plant

Most plants are green. Scientists group plants by looking at things that are similar and things that differ.

Plants have **roots**, **stems** and **leaves**.

Roots have two jobs.

1. Roots hold the plant in the ground.
2. Roots take in water to keep the plant alive.

Describe this stem.

Plants have one or more stems.

The stem holds the plant above the ground.

Suggest why some plants have **thorns**.

Leaves can trap sunlight.

Plants need sunlight to make food to grow.

Key words

roots | stems | leaves | describe | thorns

Leaf shapes

Plant leaves can look different.
They may differ in colour and shape.
This helps us to identify plants.

Leaves have veins that make different **patterns**.

Look at leaves A to F.

Can you see ways in which these leaves differ?

Look at the **edges** of the leaves.
Look at the patterns of the veins.

Use this identification key to name leaves A, B, C and D.

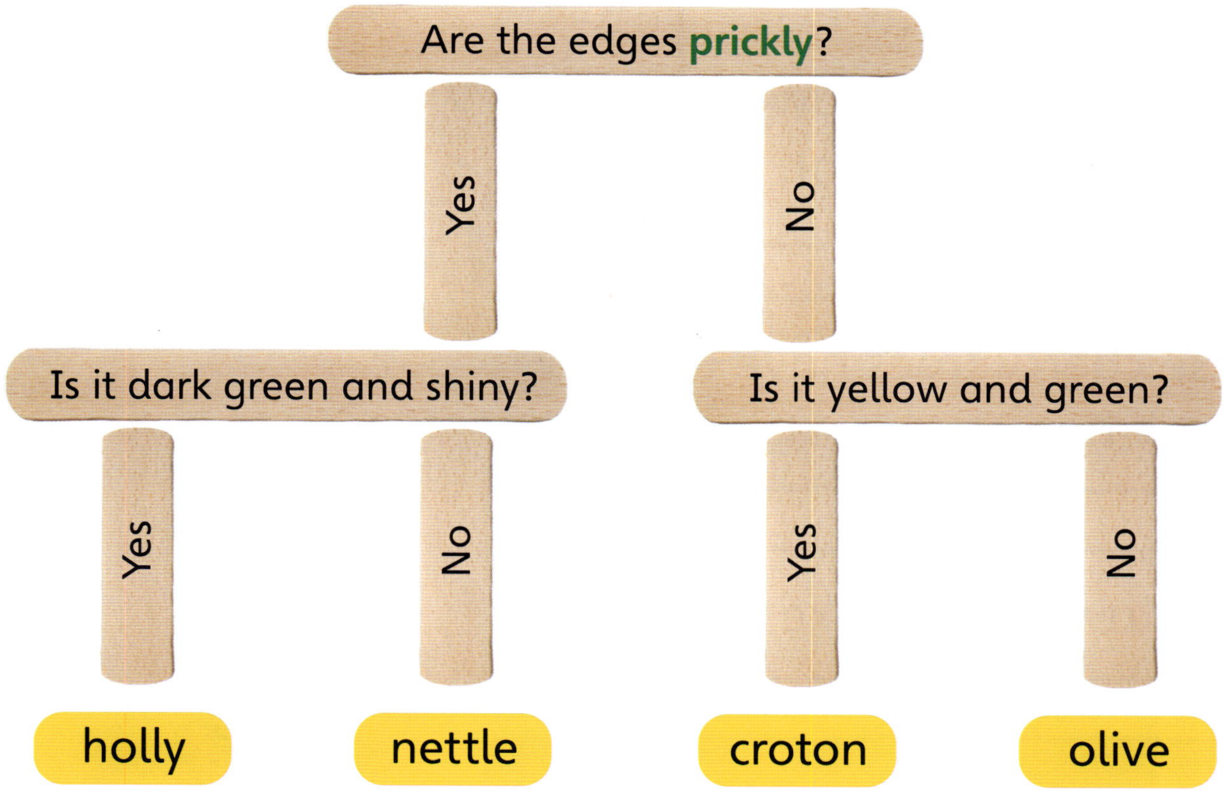

Now look at the veins, the colours and the edges of leaves that grow where you live.

Can you describe them?

Do they look like any in the pictures?

Key words

patterns

edges

prickly

Flower shapes

Many plants have flowers on them. Most plants only flower for part of each year.

These cherry trees have lots of pink flowers.

Each flower looks like this.

How many **petals** can you see?

This flower is **floating** in a pond.

Can you see its leaves?
Suggest where its roots are.

Observe flowers that grow where you live.

Look at their **shape** and colour.

Carefully remove the petals.

What shape are the petals?

What colour are they?

Look! Parts of this petal are different colours.

The yellow end joins onto the flower.

Compare the petals of the flowers you look at.

Key words

petals floating shape

Flower families

Scientists group similar flowering plants into flower **families**.

Look at these flowers from the mustard family.

How many petals do they have?

The petals make an X shape.

These flowers are from the daisy family.

The petals have similar shapes.

Do they have **more** petals or **fewer** petals than the mustard family flowers?

These are the simplest flowers in the rose family.

How many petals do they have?

Many flowers in the rose family are shaped like a bowl.

Compare the flowers in these three flower families.
How are they similar and different?

Key words

- families
- more
- fewer

Look at flowers you can see growing outside. Can you describe them?

Trees

Plants grow in different ways.
Some plants stay small and soft.

Grass grows taller as it gets older.

Trees can grow very tall.
The **woody** stem of a tree is the **trunk**.

Smaller woody parts of the stem are called **branches**.

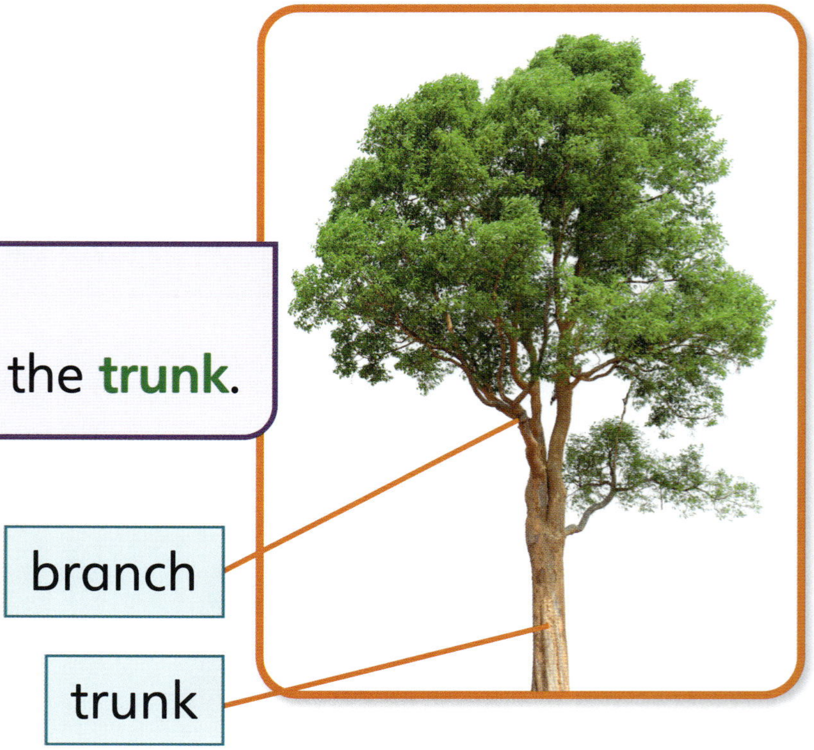

A tree trunk may have **bark** on it.

What pattern can you see inside the trunk?

Palm trees have a less woody trunk.

A palm tree trunk may look like one of these.

As the tree grows **taller** the trunk gets **wider**.

Key words

woody, trunk, branches, bark, palm, taller, wider

What are the trees like where you live?

Drawing plants

When scientists draw plants they try to show the features that help to identify the plant.

Draw with solid lines like this.
Not fuzzy lines like this.

Draw the biggest vein first.

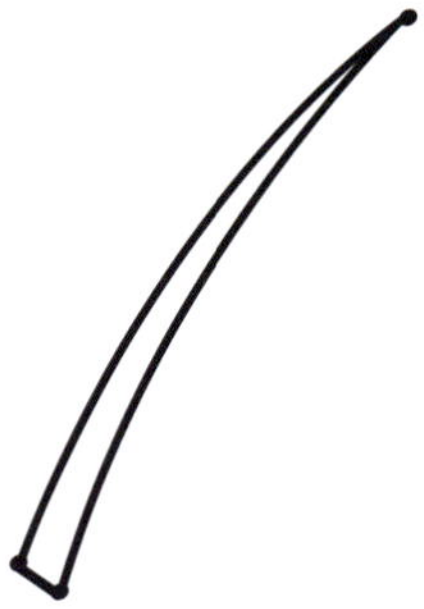

It may help to put dots to show the leaf shape first. Do not lift the **pencil** until you reach the next dot. Turn your paper so you always draw upwards to make the curve.

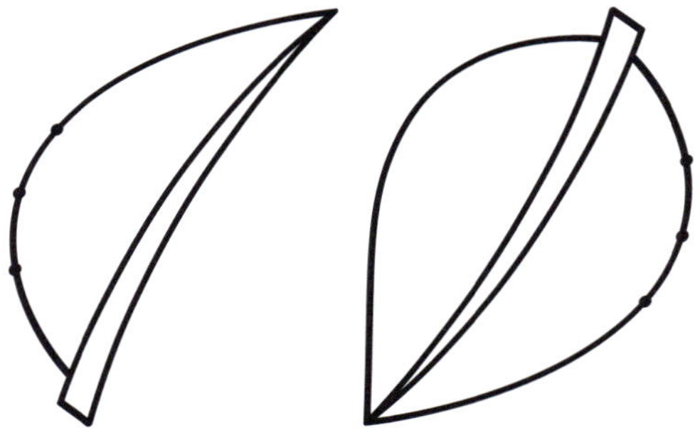

Draw the other veins.

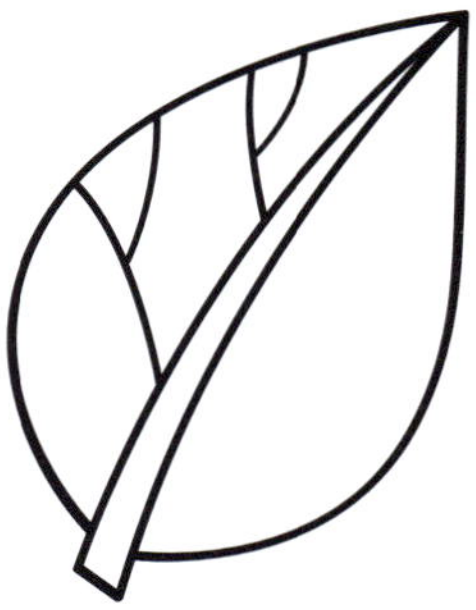

Now draw a simple flower.
Put a circle to show the **middle**.
Do not press hard.

Put dots for the petals.

Try to draw each petal the same shape.

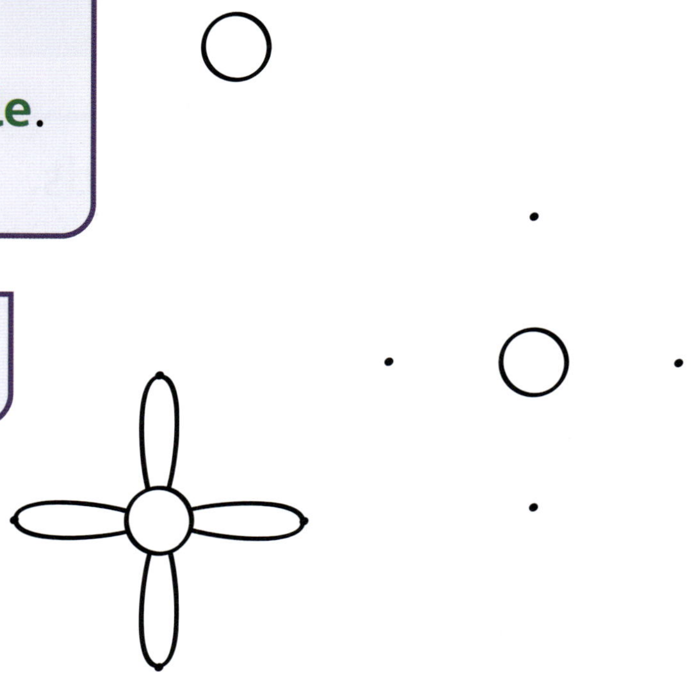

Look at the real flower to check your drawing.

You could use your finger and a brush to paint a tree branch with flowers.

Key words

pencil

middle

Seeds

Lots of plants make **seeds**.
The seeds grow into new plants.

Can you see the seeds inside these **fruits**?

We can buy packets of seeds to grow new plants.

Each packet has a picture of what the seed grows into.

We can plant the seeds ...

... in **soil** in the ground or in soil in a pot.

Now we need to give the seeds water.

Why do they need water?

They have a **food store** inside the seed.

They need water to start to use their food store to grow.

Key words

seeds | fruits | soil | food store

Bulbs

Some plants grow from **bulbs**.

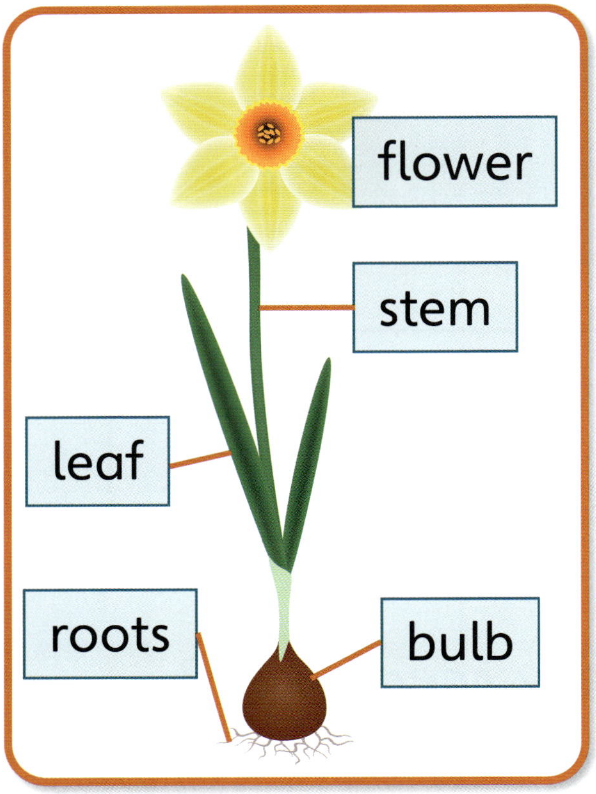

Bulbs are an **underground** food store for the plant.

Can you see roots?
Can you see leaves?

The bulb helps the plant to **survive** very cold **weather** or times when there is no rain.

Plants with bulbs can grow very quickly when the weather is better.

These flowering plants grow quickly from their bulbs while there are no leaves on the trees.

Why do they grow when there are no leaves on the trees?

The tree leaves **block** the sunlight from reaching the plants underneath.

The plants use sunlight to make food to store in their bulb for the next year.

Key words

bulbs | underground | survive | weather | block

Healthy plants

Plants need water, air and light to grow well.

Water

This plant has been given water.
It has been **watered**.

This plant has not been watered.
It has **wilted**.

Describe the wilted plant.

Air

Plants have air all around them on land.
Water plants have air in the water around them.

The picture shows air going out of a water plant. Air goes in too.

Light

Some plants need **bright** sunlight. Some plants need less light. These plants are growing towards the light.

Now their leaves can trap more sunlight.

Predict what will happen if someone turns the tray around.

Key words

watered | wilted | bright

Investigating seeds

Scientists start an **investigation** by asking a question. It must be a question they can find the answer to by doing an investigation.

Scientific question:
Do seeds need water to start to grow?

Count some seeds into two equal piles.

Put one pile of seeds on some **wet** cotton wool in a dish.

Put the other pile of seeds on some dry cotton wool in a dish.

Put the two dishes in the same place to make it a **fair test**.

Check if the wet cotton wool needs more water.

Predict which seeds will start to grow.

What is a fair test?

A fair test means you **changed** just one thing and kept everything else the same for both dishes of seeds.

What was the one thing you changed?

Think of three things you kept the **same** in both dishes.

Key words

investigation | scientific question | wet | fair test | changed | same

Growing food

Plants can provide food for humans and other animals.

Can you see crops growing in the fields?

People who grow food are called **farmers**.

The plants they grow for us to eat are called **crops**.

This farmer has **picked** some of his crops to sell.

Some farmers grow **wheat**.

Flour comes from wheat grains.

We use flour to make **bread**.

We eat lots of different parts of plants.
We eat the leaves of pak choi.

Onions are bulbs.

Oranges are fruit.

Can you see food you like to eat here?

All these foods come from plants.

Farmers grow olives for us to eat.

We can also use them to make **olive oil**.

Key words

farmers · crops · picked · wheat · flour · bread · onions · olive oil

End of topic questions

The pictures show different foods we get from plants.

Look at both sets of pictures.

1. Name as many of the foods as you can.
2. Which of the foods grow where you live?
3. Which of the foods do you like to eat?
4. Find some fruits. Which ones are berries?
5. Find some vegetables.
6. Find some nuts.

5 Sorting and grouping materials

The objects around us are made from materials.

Let us find out more about what some materials are like.

Which materials can you see in the classroom?

Many objects are made of wood, stone or glass.

Humans can make plastic in bright colours.

Our clothes are made from fabrics like wool and cotton.

Humans have used metals to make tools for thousands of years.

Wood

Everything around us is made from **materials**. **Wood** is a material we can use to make things.

Wood comes from trees. The tree trunk and big branches are cut down to make **logs**.

The logs are cut to make long, flat pieces of wood.

Humans use wood to build parts of houses ...

... and to make **furniture**.

Wood is used to make toys.

Wood can be cut into lots of shapes.

Wood can be painted different colours.

What is wood being used for here?

This person is carving wood. What do you think he is making?

What is made of wood in your classroom and at home?

Key words

materials wood logs furniture

Stone and glass

Humans have used **stone** as a **building** material for **thousands** of years.

These buildings are made of stone.

Marble is a very hard type of stone used to make **statues**.

Stone is a hard material.

This simple hut is made from stones but they are not joined together.

Can you see a stone wall behind the hut?

Glass is used to make windows.

Look for things made of stone and glass where you live.

We use glass objects at home and in science.

Which of these are used by scientists at work?

Key words

stone | building | thousands | statues | glass

Fabrics

Fabrics are **soft** materials that are used to make clothes, curtains and rugs.

Fabrics have different textures. Their **surfaces** feel different.

Which of our sense organs feels textures?

furry

smooth

rough

Cotton fabric helps to keep us **cool**.

We get cotton from plants.

Woollen fabric keeps us **warm**.

Wool comes from animals.

These animals are **goats**.

This is a **sheep**.

Look at its thick woolly coat.

Find out which other animals can give us wool.

Look for things made from different fabrics.

Are any of them cotton or wool?

Key words

fabrics | soft | surfaces | furry | smooth | rough

cotton | cool | woollen | warm | sheep | goats

Plastic

Plastic is a **human made** material.

Most plastic is made from **oil**.

Some plastics are now made in other ways.

Many people are now trying to use less plastic.

Suggest why.

glass milk bottle

What sort of bottle do you get milk in?

Which bottle do you think is better?

Why?

plastic milk bottle

Plastic can be lots of different colours.

Which bowl do you like best?

It is easy to **mould** plastic into different shapes in a **factory**.

Plastic is smooth.

It can be moulded to have a rough surface.

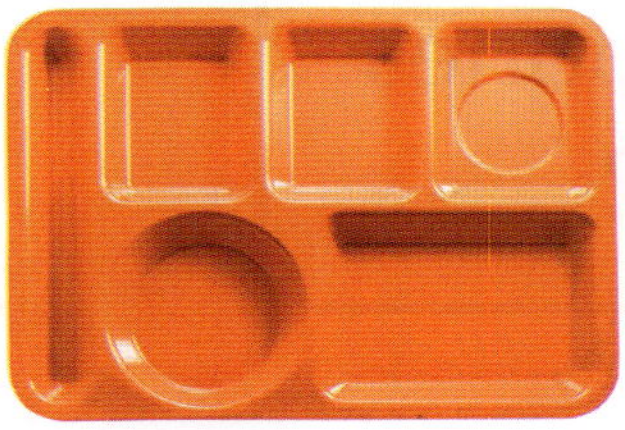

Where are the rough surfaces on these steps?

Why are these parts made rougher?

Key words

plastic | human made | oil | mould | factory

Metal

Metals are **hard** materials. Some metals are harder than others.

Titanium is a very hard metal that can be used to mend our bones.

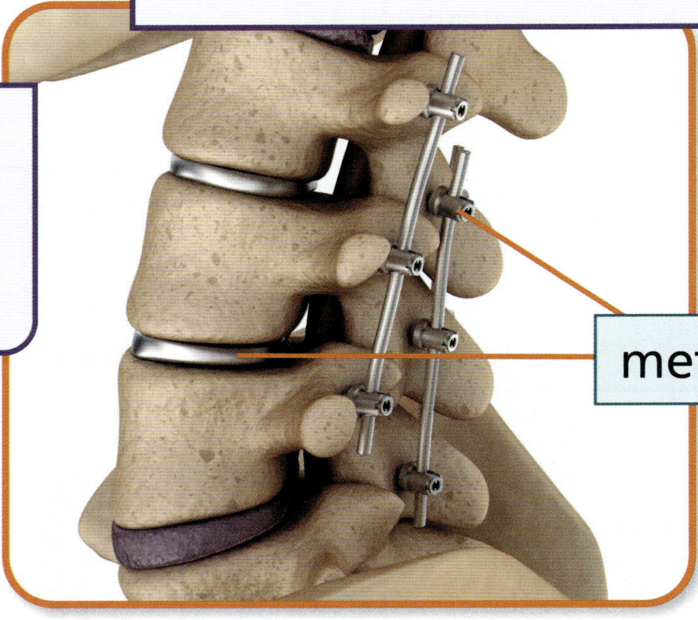

Titanium does not **bend** when we do. It holds the bones in place.

Where are these bones found in humans?

We use metals to make **tools**.

Why do tools need to be hard?

Softer metals bend **easily** into new shapes.

Gold is a metal that is used to make rings and bracelets.

Metals look very **shiny**.

Silver is used to make **jewellery** too.

Look for some metal objects in your classroom.

Are they shiny?

Are they hard?

Are they bent?

Key words

metals hard bend tools softer

easily shiny jewellery

Sorting materials

We can **sort** materials into groups.

We can sort materials by their **colour**.

red

What materials are these **red** objects made from?

rough

smooth

We can sort materials by their texture.

What materials are these objects made from?

How are these materials sorted?

Sometimes an object fits into more than one **circle**.

This scarf is blue **and** soft.
Where do I put it?

You put things that are blue **and** soft in the middle. Then they are in both circles.

Key words

sort colour red circle

Using a key for materials

We can use a key to identify animals.
We can also use a key to identify materials.

Here are some objects.
Can you identify them using the key?

You may know what all these objects are. Still work through the key to check you know how to use it.

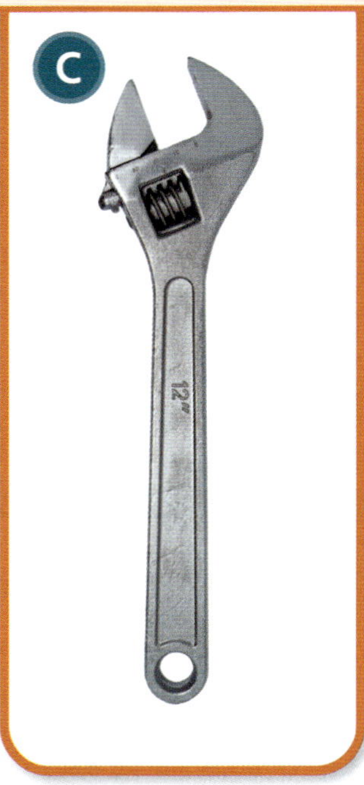

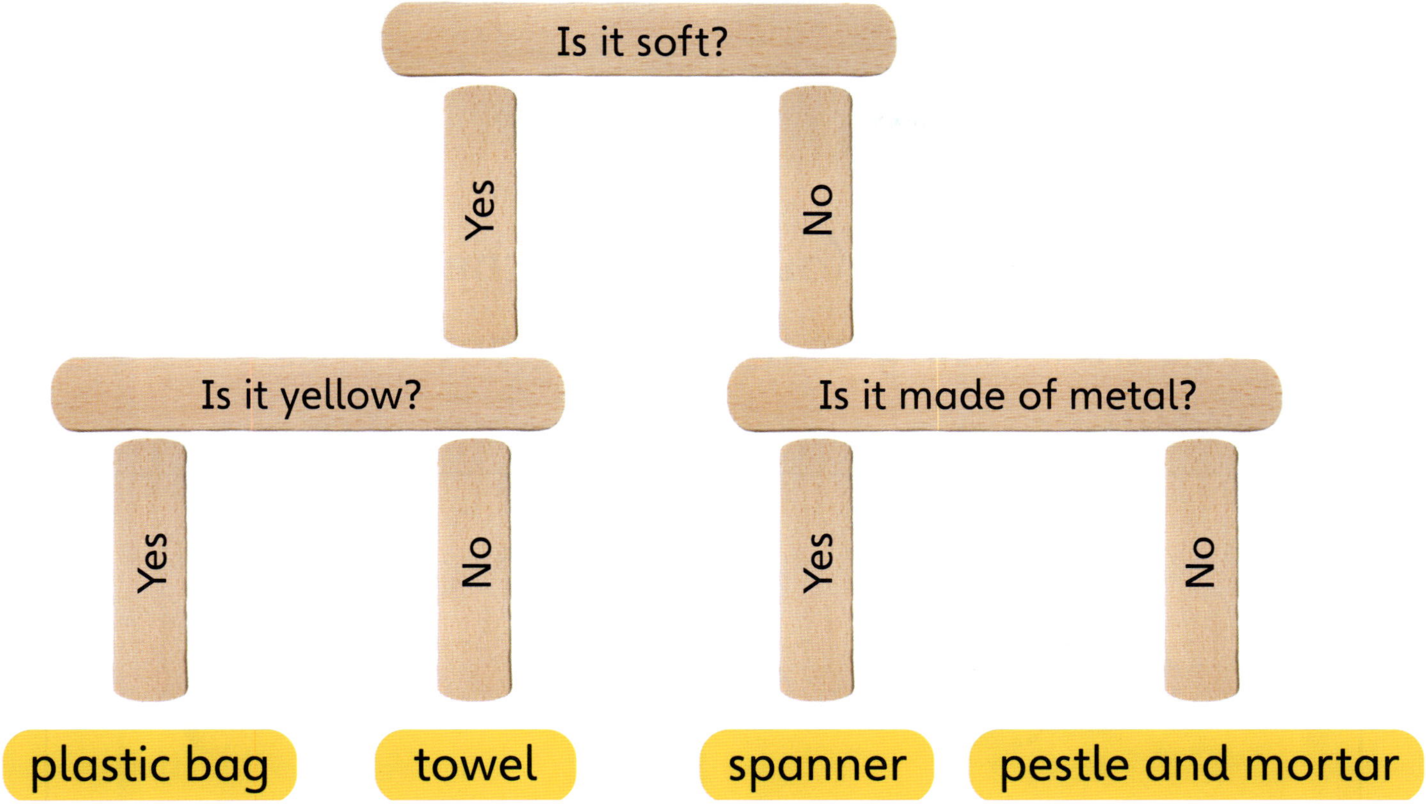

Object A is soft and blue and made of fabric.

Can you describe objects B, C and D like this?

Try making your own key for the objects in the table on page 116 of your workbook.

End of topic questions

Sorting and grouping materials

1. These objects can be found in a kitchen.
   Describe them using as many different words as you can.

 pans	 spoon
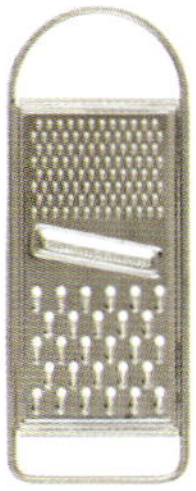 grater	 bottle
 bowl	 cloth

2 Take turns with a partner to each think of an object that is:

hard metal red

soft rough glass

smooth shiny wooden

blue stone plastic

fabric painted

6 Light and dark

Light from the Sun is all around us every day.
Light helps us to see things.
Let us find more places that light comes from.

Light comes from a source.

A light source is something that makes its own light.

Can you see three different light sources in the picture?

Sources of light

Light helps us to see things.

Where does light come from?

Light can come from different places.

Sun

lamp

light bulb

fire

torch

The place where light comes from is a source of light.

These are all **sources** of light.

A light source is something that makes its own light.

Is a **mirror** a source of light?

No, because a mirror **does not** make its own light.

What about **candles**?

Yes, a candle makes its own light. A candle is a source of light.

Key words

lamp torch sources mirror candles

What sources of light are there in your classroom?

Bright lights and dim lights

We use our eyes to sense light.

We can see the colours of objects.

In bright light we may wear **sunglasses**.

We can see the difference between bright and **dim** light.

These bright lights are called **floodlights**.

Why does this football match need floodlights?

Candles give a dim light.

The light from candles is dimmer than the light from floodlights.

Which bulb is brighter?

Which bulb is dimmer?

Inside an **aircraft** the lights are dimmed at night.

What does dim lighting help the passengers to do?

Can you see another thing that helps to dim the light?

Key words

sunglasses dim floodlights aircraft

Shiny objects

Light can **travel** through air and water. It can travel through some objects too.

Light from the Sun travels through this umbrella.

Light **bounces** off some objects. We say that these objects **reflect** light.

Shiny objects reflect a lot of light.

How is this ball made to reflect light in all directions?

The mirror reflects light from this candle.

We see a **reflection** of the candle in the mirror.

The candle is a source of light.

The mirror is **not** a source of light because it is **not** making its own light.

What shiny objects can you see around you?

Key words

travel | bounces | reflect | reflection

Light and dark

Light is all around us.

What happens when we take light away?

We get **darkness**.

Darkness is when there is no light.

It is very hard to see in darkness.

This girl is reading a book **underneath** a blanket.

Predict what will happen if she **switches** the torch off.

When you first switch a light off you cannot see anything in the dark.

But then your eyes become **adapted** to the dark.
You start to see the shapes of things.

You cannot see colours when it is dark.

We need bright light to see well.

What colours are the cushions?

The flowers are all red.

Key words

darkness | underneath | switches | adapted

Earth and Sun

We all live on **Earth**. The **Sun** is the source of light for Earth.

The Sun is very bright.

It is **dangerous** to look at the Sun because it can **damage** our eyes.

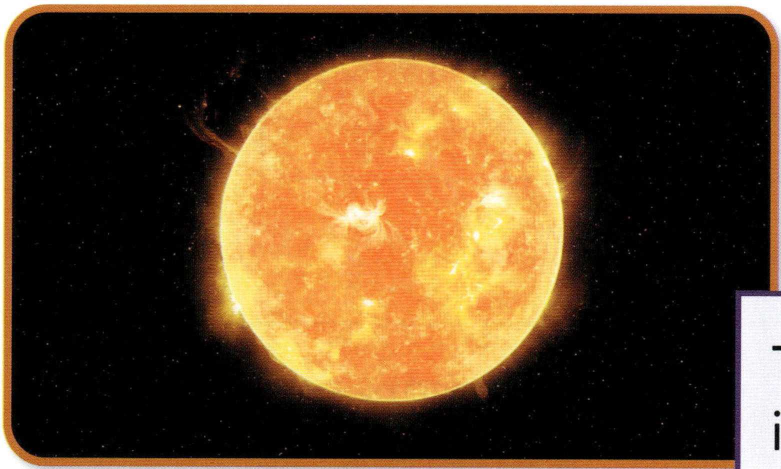

The Sun is very hot so it makes Earth warm.

Earth is a **sphere**.

Light from the Sun travels to Earth.

The other sphere is the **Moon**.

one side of Earth is light

one side of Earth is dark

Make a **model** of Earth using blue modelling clay.

Put some countries on it in another colour.

Shine a torch on your model to make the country you live in have light.

Key words

Earth · Sun · dangerous · damage · sphere · space · Moon · model

Night and day

Earth is always **turning**.

Look at a **globe**. Make it turn.

Earth turning gives us **night** and **day**.

It is day when the Sun is **shining** on the part of Earth we live on.

It is night when the Sun is shining on the other side of Earth to us.

Scientists sometimes use models to explain things.

A model is a way of showing how something works without using the real things.

In this model, the lamp represents the Sun.

The globe represents Earth.

The Sun is only shining on part of Earth.

It is day for people who live there.

What is happening on the side the Sun is **not** shining on?

Key words

turning globe night day shining

End of topic questions

Light and dark

1 a) Find two shiny objects in the picture.

b) Can you see anything that has a shiny part and a dull part?

2 The picture shows both day and night.

a) Which part shows night? Which part shows day? How do you know this?

b) What sources of light can you see in the picture?

7 Pushes and pulls

Humans move in many different ways.
We can make objects move too.
Let us see how.

We can push an object. We can pull an object.
Pushes and pulls are the forces that make objects move.

Find the toys in the picture that have wheels.

Fast and slow

Humans can move in different ways. Some movements are **fast**. Other movements are slower.

Do you think you walk faster than Victor?

Think of places you walk. When do you run?

We move faster when we run.

It takes **less** time to reach a new place.

This girl is swimming.

Which body parts help her to move in the water?

This person is climbing. She climbs slowly.

Suggest why she climbs slowly.

What is helping her to climb?

Look at her **boots**.

Look at the picture.

Predict who will jump and who will **twist**.

Key words

fast | slowly | less | boots | twist

Moving toys

Toys that move are fun to play with.

This **kite** is **flying**.

The boy is holding two **strings**.

What makes the kite move?

What makes the kite change **direction**?

These toys **spin** round in circles.

Use your hands to show how these toys move.

Will they stop moving?

This boy is **sitting** on a **seesaw**.

What will make the seesaw move?

Which way will the boy move?

This girl has a **bicycle**.

How does she make the bicycle move?

Use your hands to show how the **wheels** move.

Do you have any toys that move? How do they move?

Key words

kite   flying   strings   direction   spin

sitting   seesaw   bicycle   wheels

Starting to move

Objects need a **push** or a **pull** to start them moving.

The boy is lying down in a ball pool.

The balls are not moving.

What happens when he jumps up?

This swing needs a **force** to start it moving.

If someone pushes the swing it will start to move.

Pushes and pulls are forces.

Objects will only move if there is a force acting on them.

The bowling pins are not moving.

When the ball hits the pins it makes them move.

The moving ball is a pushing force.

Key words

push

pull

force

What other sports use pushing forces to make something start to move?

Pushes and pulls

Pushes and pulls are forces that make objects move.

A push is when you move an object **away** from you.

push

push

A pull is when you move an object **towards** you.

pull

pull

A push can make an object move.

The bigger the push, the bigger the force.

A bigger push makes the girl swing higher.

Discuss these pictures with a partner.

Which people are pulling and which people are pushing?

Key words

away

towards

Moving in circles

Some objects always move in circles.

The hands on this clock move in circles.
We say the hands move **clockwise**.

This sign tells drivers to go clockwise around a roundabout.

This one tells drivers to go **anticlockwise**.

Which way does the boy push the wheels to move forwards?

Clockwise or anticlockwise?

Have you seen a ride like this?

People sit in the coloured pods.

The white pod moves down.

Which way is the wheel **turning**?

Which way is the roundabout moving?

How is the girl making it move?

Key words

- clockwise
- anticlockwise
- turning

Can you think of other things that move in circles?

End of topic questions

1 How are these children moving?
Discuss your ideas with a partner.

2 Write a list of all the ways that you can move.